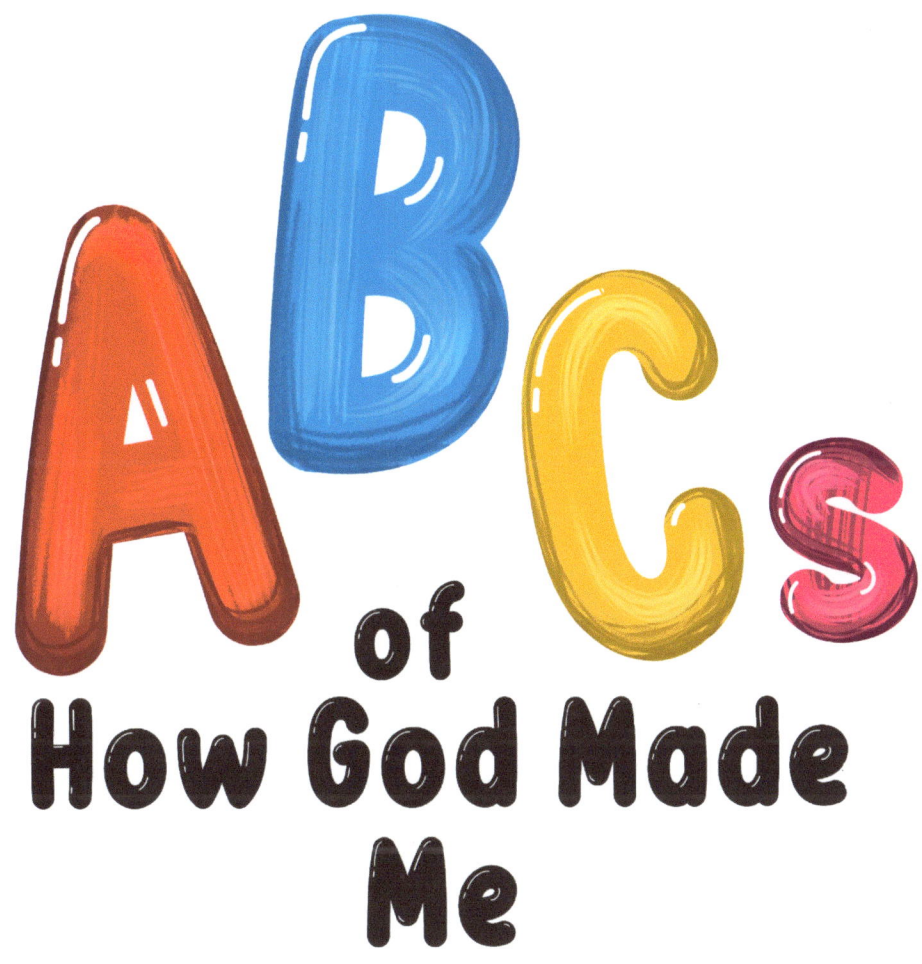

ABCs of How God Made Me

Written by:
Sunny Kang

Illustrated by:
Alexandro Ockyno

Text and Illustrations Copyright © 2021 Sunny Kang
All rights reserved. No part of this publication may be reproduced, distributed, or transmitted in any form or by any means, including photocopying, recording, or other electronic or mechanical methods, without the prior written permission of the publisher, except in the case of brief quotations embodied in reviews and certain other non-commercial uses permitted by copyright law.
The moral right of the author and illustrator has been asserted.
Cover design and illustrations by Alexandro Ockyno

Paperback: 978-1-7363548-3-4
Hardcover: 978-1-7363548-4-1
E-Book: 978-1-7363548-5-8

To You Who Are Fearfully & Wonderfully Made,

Allow God to tell you how AMAZING He made YOU to be!

To :

From :

Date :

Before God created the world,

In His mind,

God made me...

F is for Favored!

Favored means to be chosen above others.

People like me and choose me time and time again.
I thank God for favor from different people and friends.

P is for Patient!

Patience is when you are good at waiting.

The greatest blessings can take time.
By waiting patiently
my blessings multiply.

S is for Strong!

Strong is having much strength.

I am strong enough to carry my lunch and book bag too.
I can even carry some of your sadness if you need me to.

U is for Unique!

Unique means special or one of a kind.

Like snowflakes are one of a kind,
No one has my shape, size, and mind combined.

V is for Valuable!

Valuable means to have value or importance.

I am valuable and important because God said. Jesus is my Lord and He calls me His friend.

Y is for Young!

Young means newer or fresher.

I am young in my body, heart, and mind. When I am old, I will still be young and child-like inside.

Z is for Zealous!

Zealous is having a lot of passion or desire for something.

When I find something I like, I give it my all. God is my passion every winter, spring, summer, and fall!

About the Author and Illustrator

Author
Sunny Kang is a Christ follower, husband, father, teacher, preacher, and author. He has pastored for over 10 years, serving as children's pastor for several of those years.
He enjoys learning, meeting new people, communicating God's Word, superhero movies, and boba! He, his wife, and 2 sons live and serve in Las Vegas.

Follow Author:
Facebook: @AuthorSunnyKang
Instagram: @AuthorSunnyKang
Newsletter: http://bit.ly/authorsunnykang

Illustrator
Alexandro Ockyno is a full time freelance illustrator, living in Bali for almost 9 years. A happy man with a beautiful girlfriend, his dream is to create many children's books and share God's blessings with many others.

Follow Author:
Facebook: @alessandro.altobelly
Instagram: @catandsashimi

DOWNLOAD YOUR FREE GIFT HERE!

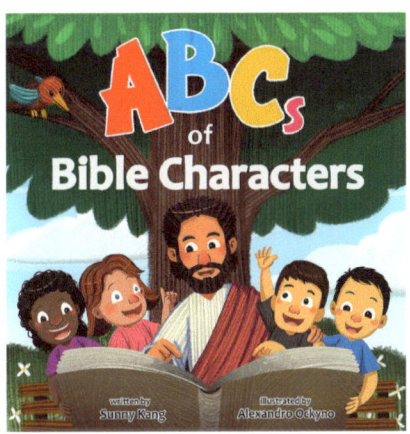

Link: https://bit.ly/ABCs-Of-Bible-Characters-FreePDF

www.ingramcontent.com/pod-product-compliance
Lightning Source LLC
Chambersburg PA
CBHW041713160426
43209CB00018B/1819